More People Like Us

BERYL BYE

Falcon Books. London

First published 1972
© Beryl J. Bye 1972
Illustrations: Alan Denyer

Overseas agents

EMU Book Agencies Ltd, 511 Kent Street, NSW, Australia

CSSM and Crusader Bookroom Society Ltd, 177 Manchester Street, Christchurch, New Zealand

Sunday School Centre Wholesale, PO Box 3020, Cape Town, South Africa

Published by CPAS Publications, a department of the Church Pastoral Aid Society, Falcon Court, 32 Fleet Street, London EC4Y 1DB

Made and printed by
Redwood Press Limited, Trowbridge, Wiltshire

Contents

Fiona the Nurse
    South American Missionary Society   7

Cliff the Singer
    The Crusaders' Union   37

June the Doctor
    Overseas Missionary Fellowship   61

Jeanette the Captain
    Salvation Army   79

To my readers

People Like Us was a book of true stories about men and women who are teaching people about the Lord Jesus Christ and at the same time doing a job that is useful to the community.

More People Like Us is a follow-on book which tells the stories of four more people who have trusted in the Lord Jesus for the forgiveness of their sins and now want to use their lives in serving Him, and telling other people about Him.

They are all real people, and I have used their real Christian names in the stories. One is a doctor, treating patients who are ill with leprosy in Thailand; one is a well-known singer who uses the talent God has given him to put over the Christian message in song; one is a Salvation Army captain who is helping to make a home for young people who have been in some kind of trouble; and one is a nurse working in South America.

All of these people are quite young, and all of them thoroughly enjoy the jobs to which they feel God has called them, and for which they have been trained.

On the contents page I have listed the societies and organizations with whom these people work. If you are specially interested in any of them you could find out more about their work from the societies concerned, so that you could pray regularly for them, and perhaps discover other ways in which you could help them.

Beryl Bye

Fiona the Nurse

The long, wailing moan of the air raid siren disturbed little Fiona in her sleep and she moved her head restlessly. Before she was properly awake her mother had scooped her up from her cot, wrapped her in a blanket and carried her downstairs. As she sleepily rubbed her eyes, she could hear her older brother crying fretfully. Fiona could never understand why William cried when the sirens went. She found it rather exciting to climb into the Anderson air-raid shelter that was built under the dining-room table, and to drink hot chocolate in the middle of the night.

Fiona was too little to understand what it all meant, but William understood—a little—and that was why he cried.

One night when they were all huddled together under the dining-room table there was a big crash! It was quite the loudest noise Fiona had ever heard. It made her mother put her arms tightly round her baby daughter and exchange worried glances with her husband. It sounded as if the house was falling down.

'It's one of those doodle-bugs', her father said softly. 'I'm afraid someone has copped it. And not so far away either. We're lucky it missed us'.

Fiona didn't know that a 'doodle-bug' was a

large bomb. It was fitted with a motor that was capable of carrying it a considerable distance under its own power. Then the engine was timed to 'cut out', and the bomb dived to the earth carrying its huge charge of explosives with it.

When it was light, Fiona's father went to find out where the bomb had fallen. Half of the houses in the road had been destroyed, and there was rubble everywhere.

'You and the children must go somewhere safer', Fiona's father said to her mother. 'You can't stay here. Next time it may be us'.

'But what about you?' Fiona's mother asked anxiously.

'I can't just walk out', he answered, 'I've my work to do. There's going to be plenty of jobs for a builder before this war is over. Besides, there's the Home Guard. I may be too old for the Services, but I can still do my bit home here'.

'But where shall we go?' Fiona's mother said doubtfully.

'You can go to Helen's', her father said. 'She's got a job as Catering Officer at a Land Army Hostel in Badger. I'm sure she'll find room for you somewhere. You can't stay here anyway—that's clear'.

Aunt Helen made them very welcome. She arranged for them to live with the gardener and his wife in their little cottage, in the grounds of the big house that had been taken over as a Hostel for girls of the Land Army. The girls of the Land Army were trained to do many of the farming jobs that had previously been done by men. They learned to plough and harrow and plant; looked after the animals and kept the fences and hedges in good repair.

When she was four years old Fiona started going to school. There were some American soldiers living in the village. They came from the big Army Camp not far away. They loved the children at the village school and became very friendly with them. Fiona was a favourite with Benny—a tall young soldier with twinkling blue eyes.

'When I get home again and this war is over, I'll send you the biggest doll that money can buy', he promised the little girl.

'Will it have eyes that close?' Fiona wanted to know.

'It certainly will', the young soldier promised.

Benny never forgot his promise. In 1945 when the war was over, a huge parcel arrived for Fiona from America. In the parcel was a simply enormous doll. It was just like a small baby, and it had eyes that closed when you laid it down.

By this time Fiona and her mother and brother were back home in Beckenham. At first she went to a church called St. John's. On Saturday mornings throughout the holidays, St. John's ran a Holiday Special, and Fiona and her friend Margaret went along every week. The team of grown-ups who organized the Holiday Special was headed by a man who told the children to call him Uncle Michael. Fiona liked him very much, and listened spellbound as he told them stories about Jesus, and talked to them about what it meant to be a Christian.

'How many of you are going to ask the Lord Jesus to come into your hearts and be your very own Saviour ?' Uncle Michael asked the children as the end of the holidays and Holiday Special drew near.

'I am', Fiona whispered to herself, and before she went home she told Uncle Michael what she had decided to do. He was very pleased and talked to her for a long time, making sure that she really understood the big step that she had decided to take.

A year later her family moved to another part of Beckenham. Fiona had to leave St. John's Church and joined Christchurch—which was the mother church of St. John's. Christchurch had a Youth Club, and Fiona became a member.

One day a missionary from Pakistan came to speak to them. She was a nurse, and Fiona was very interested in all she had to say. When she got home she spoke to her parents.

'I've decided what I want to be when I grow up', she said. 'I'm going to be a nurse'.

'Well, that's all right', her father said. 'Nursing is quite a good career for a woman, but it's very hard work'.

'I'm not going to be an ordinary nurse', Fiona went on firmly. 'I'm going to be a missionary, and go out to other lands to tell people about God'.

'Oh, I expect you'll change your mind a dozen times during the next few years', her mother said comfortably. 'It's a long time before you'll be finished with school and have to start thinking about a job'.

'It's this convent she's going to', her father said to her mother privately. 'It's putting too many religious ideas into the girl's head'.

Her new convent school did impress Fiona in many ways, but it had nothing to do with the ideas of her life work that were gradually forming themselves in Fiona's head. It was true she did think, briefly, about becoming a nun.

'They always look so still and peaceful', she confided to her best friend. 'And I love to see them kneeling before the altar in their black and white habits. They look so holy somehow and set apart. I'd like to look like that too'.

But young Fiona was certainly not prepared for the rigid discipline that was thrust upon you if you became a nun.

'How are you sure you are going to Heaven?' she asked one of the teaching nuns after a lesson in which some of the teaching of the Catholic Church had been discussed.

'Because I am a nun', the woman explained patiently.

'But that's rubbish!' Fiona exploded to her friends during break. 'It doesn't say in the Bible that you go to heaven just because you are a nun! You go to heaven because you have faith in the Lord Jesus Christ, and for no other reason'.

Some of Fiona's opinions got back to the Mother

Superior, and one day she took Fiona aside and gave her a straight talking to.

'If you are going to rebel so much against the Church, it might be better if you left', she said. 'The Sisters tell me you are always arguing and asking difficult questions'.

Fiona was thinking about leaving school anyway. She had been attending regular Bible studies at her Church, was a keen member of the Young People's Fellowship, and went to church services each week. She read her Bible each day with the help of Scripture Union notes, and altogether was beginning to have a very clear idea of what was involved in being a Christian.

'I've had enough of the Convent', she told her parents, one evening when she was about sixteen. 'I don't agree with what they teach us anyway, so what's the use of staying on? I still want to be a nurse, but I can't start my training until I'm eighteen and a half, so I might as well do something else in the meantime'.

Fiona left school and enrolled for a course of shorthand, typing, book-keeping and general subjects at Pitman's College in Lewisham. Two years later she applied for a secretarial job in London and became secretary to the Manager of the Water and Boilermakers' Association.

Although Fiona quite enjoyed her job and was pretty good at it, it was still only the means to an end. It was a way of filling time until she was old enough to start a nursing course.

She was going through a period of testing over her Christian faith at this time. She had become friendly with a young married couple and one night after a Communion service Fiona was very thoughtful.

She couldn't help noticing the expression of joy and love that was on Jean's face throughout the service.

'It obviously means an awful lot to her', Fiona thought to herself. 'Why don't I feel like that about it ? To me it's just a service of remembering and not much more. It almost makes me wonder if I'm really a Christian'.

Fiona worried about the question for the next three days and at last she told Jean and Mick all about it.

'Feelings can't be relied upon', Mick reminded her. 'You must know that. You are a Christian because you've asked the Lord Jesus Christ into your heart and life, and that's the only standard you need to measure by. We're all different and we feel differently about different things. You can't expect to be a carbon copy of Jean any more than Jean will ever be exactly like you'.

But Fiona wasn't satisfied. She was secretly tormented by the thought 'Am I a Christian or not ? If so, why doesn't the Communion service mean as much to me as it does to Jean ?'

The subject really began to prey on her mind. One day she went for a long walk determined to sort things out.

'There's nothing more I can do, Lord', she prayed silently as she strode along. 'If I'm not right with You in any way—then please put things right'.

Suddenly Fiona felt a wonderful feeling of peace and freedom. She was not the first person to go through the experience of worrying over the free gift of salvation that had already been given to her —and of worrying without a cause.

Now things began to speed up. Fiona was eighteen and a half, the time had come to apply to a hospital for enrolment as a student nurse. She applied to a hospital in Tunbridge Wells and it was agreed that she should start in October 1957.

Fiona has never forgotten how nervous she felt as she presented herself at the Sister Tutor's office on that first day of her nursing career, and how relieved she was when she saw a Scripture Union badge pinned to the lapel of one of the other student nurses with whom she was to share a dormitory.

'My name's Jenny, what's yours?' the owner of

the badge asked, when they were alone for the first time.

'I'm Fiona. I was glad to see your badge', Fiona confessed. 'I thought I might be the only Christian around here'.

Later Fiona found that their two principal tutors were Christians as well.

Fiona had been nursing a secret fear about starting her nursing training.

'It's all right being a Christian when you are mixing with lots of other people who feel the same way as you do', she had reasoned with herself. 'And when you've got a keen church where you can always find people of the same mind. But shall I be able to stand firmly when I'm pitchforked into the middle of a new life, when everything is going to be completely different, and I may not find any other Christians around?'

Now it was as if the Lord was saying to Fiona, 'Don't worry! I'll see that you have fellowship with other Christians. My people are to be found everywhere. There's no need to be afraid'.

Fiona settled down to hospital work very happily. She hadn't forgotten about her earlier wish to become a missionary nurse, but she knew that there was nothing she could do about the idea until she had finished her training. It was about this time that she read about five missionaries who had been martyred in South America, and she thought a lot about them. Somehow she couldn't get the matter out of her mind. South America came to the forefront of her thoughts and prayers. 'Is God telling me that one day he wants me to serve Him in South America?' she wondered. 'Perhaps this is the way he speaks to people—by planting the seed of a thought in their minds and just leaving it to grow'.

Fiona had always imagined that a Christian nurse would have lots of opportunities of talking to the patients about the Lord Jesus Christ, but most of the time she was too busy making beds and emptying bedpans, and changing dressings to have time to talk at all! It was not until well into her second year that she had her first real chance to offer help and comfort to someone who was dangerously ill.

One of her patients was a big, good-looking man of thirty-five. He was married and had two children, and he was incurably ill with cancer of the spine. As the weeks went on, he realized that he was not getting any better, and he began to suspect that the true nature of his illness was being kept from him. One morning, when Fiona was settling him, he caught her wrist to detain her.

'Rosey', he said urgently. 'You must tell me. Am I going to die?'

Fiona hesitated. Only a doctor has the authority to discuss his illness with a patient. Sometimes remarkable recoveries took place, when it appeared that there was little or no chance of a patient getting better, so it was very difficult to be quite sure of the outcome of a disease.

'Are you afraid to die?' Fiona asked gently, not answering the man's question outright.

'No', he replied, 'at least I don't think I am. But I must know one way or the other, nurse. I feel that everyone is hiding the truth from me, and I've just got to be told'.

Fiona prayed to God for guidance, then she said, 'You are very, very ill. No one can be sure, but it seems unlikely that you will ever be well again'.

'Thank you', the big man said quietly, releasing Fiona's wrist and sinking back slowly against his pillows. 'Thank you for being honest with me. Now I know where I stand'.

Fiona sat down beside his bed.

'There's so much I must put right', he said, half to himself. 'My wife, for instance. I've been dreadful to my wife. All this time she must have known, and yet had to keep it to herself. And I only thought of my own pain and distress—never of hers'.

'I'm sure she has understood', Fiona comforted him.

'I used to go to church, you know, nurse', he went on reflectively, 'when I was younger. But somehow I haven't bothered very much over the last few years. But I do believe in Christ and I am sure that I shall soon go to be with Him'.

She talked to the young man for a while, and prayed with him, for himself and his family. She read to him from the 23rd Psalm too, and gradually the face which had, over the past weeks, become drawn with pain, became relaxed and peaceful.

'I'd like to see my wife', he said at last. What they said to each other would always remain a secret, for he died peacefully, later that day. Fiona was glad she had told him the truth.

In September 1960 Fiona passed her hospital Final exams. Confidently in October she sat her State Final exams, and failed miserably. She was naturally very disappointed, and particularly as she and another girl had already applied to go to Hammersmith Hospital in London to take a midwifery course.

Fiona wasn't sure why she had decided on Hammersmith. Jenny had tried to dissuade her.

'Why don't you come to Woolwich with me, Fiona?' she had asked. 'Woolwich is an excellent hospital with a tremendoous Christian background. It will be wonderful to work in an atmosphere like that'.

'No thanks, Jenny', Fiona had said. 'Sue has applied for Hammersmith. I've decided to do the same'.

'Why have you applied to Hammersmith particularly?' the Christian Sister Tutor asked Fiona one day.

Fiona shrugged. 'No special reason, Sister', she confessed. 'But I thought it was as good as anywhere else'.

In March 1961 Fiona sat her State Final examination again, and again she failed. This time she felt considerably more concerned. Sister sent for her when the results came out.

'I can't understand the examination results, nurse', she said. 'From the nursing point of view there is no reason at all for you to fail'. She paused. 'I want to speak to you as a fellow Christian and not as a tutor now', she said.

Fiona wondered what was coming.

'Sometimes God closes doors when we are not "in His will",' she reminded Fiona. 'Do you think that He is perhaps closing the door to Hammersmith Hospital to you? You will have to withdraw your application anyway in view of your exam results. You can take the exam for the third and final time in June. In the meantime, I suggest you think and pray very carefully about your future plans'.

Fiona had the good sense to follow the Sister Tutor's advice. She prayed very earnestly, and, very gradually, she began to feel that she should apply, not for a Midwifery Course, but for Sick Children's Nursing Training.

She applied to three hospitals but the reply she had from the Westminster Children's Hospital was the most friendly, and she and her friend Sue were accepted to begin training in January 1962.

For the third time Fiona took her State Nursing Finals, and this time, to her great relief, she passed. She and Sue moved to the nurses' home of the Westminster Children's Hospital and started their twelve months training for Sick Children's Nurse.

Fiona had not forgotten about her decision to become a missionary, and she felt that the time had now come when she should do something about it, so she applied to a Bible College, for she knew she would need Bible training to equip her for the work ahead. She provisionally booked a place for the autumn of 1965.

Meanwhile things were going well. When Fiona took her first set of preliminary exams on children's nursing she came top of the list—it seemed to her almost as if God were saying, 'Now you are walking in the path I have chosen for you'.

At the end of 1962 Fiona again began to think about the future.

The thought of the Maternity Hospital at Woolwich was still churning around at the back of Fiona's mind. Judy and Sheila, two Christian nurses who had taken their midwifery training there, were full of praise for the place.

'The Matron is an absolute sweetie', Judy told Fiona and Sue. 'And most of the sisters are Christians too. Every time a baby is delivered the midwife prays a prayer of thanksgiving for the safe delivery, and there are special services in the little chapel each morning for the staff, and services for the patients as well'.

'The chapel was built first, and then the rest of the hospital was built round it', Sheila put in. 'The idea is that you feel that God is really at the centre of things'.

Sue was vaguely interested, and Fiona more so. They both knew that Woolwich was considered a very good training hospital, and they were both keen to get their midwifery qualification, and so in the spring of 1963, after they had taken and passed their State exam, they applied for training and were accepted for October of the same year.

Life in the hospital at Woolwich seemed quite different from an ordinary hospital, and yet it was difficult to put your finger on exactly where the differences lay. They were both very impressed by Matron, who seemed to have a real and personal interest in every nurse and patient in the hospital. They couldn't get used to the fact that everyone was so polite, either! It seemed almost too good to be true. People went out of their way to be kind, and there was no swearing at all. There was a very happy and close relationship between the nurses and the patients too. From the moment that a patient entered the hospital she was put in the special charge of a particular pupil midwife, who cared for her from that time onwards. Fiona began to understand why the hospital was held up as a model, and talked about throughout the country.

One special incident stands out in Fiona's mind about her happy stay at Woolwich. It happened when she had the terrifying but exciting task of delivering her very first baby into the world. Her hands were shaking so much that she could hardly control them! Suddenly she felt the warm firm, confident hands of the Christian Sister cover her own, guiding them and steadying them. Immediately Fiona felt her own confidence return. She never forgot that moment.

'Every time I deliver a baby', she will tell you, 'I feel those guiding hands over mine. It gave me a spiritual lesson too. When we lack confidence, God's hands covering ours can supply all the strength we need'.

And still Fiona's training went on. In June 1964 she was off to Bristol to do her Part 2 Midwifery training 'on the district'. This meant visiting people in their own homes and delivering the babies there too. First she did the rounds with a trained midwife, but after watching and helping at the deliveries, Fiona was allowed to attend mothers on her own. When the time came to take her Part 2 State exams, at the end of 1964, Fiona passed with flying colours. Now it was time to think of Bible College again. For the first time Fiona began to have doubts about the place she had provisionally booked. The year before, while at Woolwich, she had met a girl called Lynn, who was a nurse about to go to St. Michael's College, at Oxford, for her Bible training before going abroad as a missionary.

'What Society are you going out with?' she asked Lynn.

'The South American Missionary Society—you know, SAMS', Lynn said. 'They have a great need of nurses; why don't you write to them for some information?'

But Fiona was doubtful.

'I've already fixed up to go to a Bible college', she said. 'Do SAMS people usually go to St. Mike's?'

'A lot of them do', Lynn agreed. 'But I should write to SAMS anyway'.

But Fiona didn't write—not for a while.

'There's no great hurry', she thought to herself, 'and I'm fixed up for the next two years anyway'.

But in 1964, when Fiona had finally completed her very long training—first as a State Registered Nurse, then as a Children's Nurse, and finally as a Midwife, she decided one day to write to the South American Missionary Society—just to find out what it was all about.

At Christmas they invited her to an interview. As Fiona entered the office she suddenly felt completely at home. It was almost as if she heard God saying to her, 'This is the way, walk ye in it'.

The interviewing officer kept Fiona a long time.

'How did you first become interested in South America?' he wanted to know.

Fiona told him about the five martyred missionaries whose story had stayed with her throughout the years.

'How did you become a Christian? What are your qualifications? Where do you plan to do your Bible training?' the questions went on, one after the other, until Fiona began to feel slightly dazed.

'Well', the SAMS interviewer said at last, 'you seem to be the kind of person that we're looking for. But I'm not sure about your training. Do you feel any particular leading to that college?'

Fiona shook her head. 'I didn't think it mattered at the time', she confessed. 'One college seemed to be as good as another. Now I'm beginning to think I should have prayed and thought more carefully about it'.

'If you go to St. Michael's at Oxford you would only need one year's training instead of two', Fiona's new friend pointed out.

'I think I'll give them a ring now, and see what the position is for entry next April. If they are full up we shall have to think again'.

But this was obviously, for Fiona, the right way. In response to the phone call, the Principal of St Michael's interviewed Fiona without delay and she was finally accepted for a year's training from April 1965.

From September to November 1966 she went to Allen Gardiner House at Tunbridge Wells for an Orientation Course, to prepare her for the rather primitive life that she would be leading in South America. She learned to do the most extraordinary things—very far removed from nursing! Things like renewing washers of taps, putting up brick walls, and learning how to deal with the mechanical side of a car. She even did some carpentry, and was quite proud of a set of bookshelves which she put up in the library.

Fiona was to smile later, as she recalled some of the training. She had learned how to change the ballcock in a lavatory system for instance—but 'lavatories' in South America consisted of holes in the ground! There were very few taps either, so the need to change washers didn't occur very often! They learned cooking as well, and haircutting—practising on the men at the Orientation Centre, who had mixed feelings when they examined the result in the mirror afterwards!

The time passed very quickly, and in December 1966 Fiona prepared to spend her last Christmas at home before embarking by ship for South America in February 1967 with another girl—Joyce.

The first day out the ship ran into a storm. It was very severe, and the ship was blown twenty-four hours off course. All the rest of her fellow missionaries, and most of the passengers, huddled in their bunks suffering from seasickness, but Fiona felt wonderful! She stayed on deck, and revelled in the fury of the wind and waves. To her own surprise she wasn't frightened! Dressed in thick shoes and a heavy raincoat, she braved the storm and turned up in the nearly empty dining-room at meal times ready to tuck into a hearty dinner!

When they docked at Buenos Aires they were met by Barbara and Michael. Barbara had come specially from the north to meet Fiona and Joyce and take them to Algarrobal where they were to work. The first part of the journey was by train which stopped for a while at Rosario where some Christian university students were waiting to welcome the new missionaries.

On the train went, and at one o'clock the next day they arrived in Tucuman and Fiona's long journey was nearly over. A luxury coach met the train. It had reclining seats and a hostess to serve cool drinks. Fiona felt like a rich girl on a luxury tour and not a missionary about to take up her first posting!

At Salta they were met by the SAMS Field Superintendent Bill, and his secretary, Val.

'Excuse me limping,' Val apologized, 'I trod on a snake ten days ago and it's still painful. It will teach me to look where I'm going next time'.

Fiona gulped. She watched very carefully where she put her feet! That night Joyce, Barbara and Fiona stayed at an hotel in Salta. Bill and Val joined them for supper in a restaurant. Fiona didn't feel very hungry after her long journey, so she had salad. Later she was to wish that she had chosen something that had been cooked! Next day they went on by road in a SAMS jeep to Algarrobal.

As the journey progressed they all got very hot and dusty and were soon dripping with perspiration. Fiona was also feeling queasy in her tummy, but she put it down to the excitement.

On their arrival at Algarrobal Fiona realized how the Queen must feel when hundreds of people line up to shake hands. Everyone turned out to greet them—about two hundred in all. Joyce and Fiona were shown to the little house where they were to live. It was a small, two-roomed bungalow with a tin roof and mud-brick walls, and suddenly Fiona was anxious to get inside and realized she didn't feel like a brave new missionary any more. She began to feel very, very ill.

Beryl, the nurse from the dispensary, came and diagnosed dysentry—a very severe form of sickness and diarrhoea. 'I expect it was the salad', she remarked after questioning Fiona about what she had eaten during the last twenty-four hours. 'I'm afraid it's better to steer off anything that hasn't been boiled here—unless you wash it yourself. I'll give you an injection and then you'll soon feel better'.

But Fiona didn't really feel herself again for nearly a week. She felt it was a very unfortunate beginning to her life as a missionary nurse!

After a few weeks Fiona went back to Rosario to learn Spanish. She stayed at the American Methodist College there and Sylvia who was an Argentinian teacher came every day to give her lessons. Sometimes she went to Sylvia's home and sometimes she attended the General and Maternity Hospitals in Rosario just to watch what was going on. The doctors were very helpful and allowed Fiona to accompany them on their rounds, explaining things very slowly in Spanish so that Fiona could learn the medical terms. She went to some of the lectures at the School of Nursing as well, taking any chance that came her way to hear the language being spoken.

At last, after six months hard study, Fiona felt she was ready to begin her real work. She was posted to Juarez—a small railway town with 2,500 people and two Indian villages, one on the north side of the town, and one on the south.

'Your job is not to set up a rival hospital', Fiona was told, 'but to encourage the hospital in the town to take the Indian patients who need treatment, and to persuade the Indians to overcome their natural fears and attend the hospital. You will not stay in Juarez all the time. Your work will mean travelling out to the Indian villages, and the cotton and sugar-cane fields where the Indians work, and getting to know them there. Sometimes you will be away three or four weeks at a time'.

Life was very different from the planned routine of an English teaching hospital. Fiona and her fellow nurse, Lois, would set off in the jeep, heavily laden with food, water, petrol, medicines, cooking equipment and sleeping bags. They would take with them a male Indian to escort them on the journey. Sometimes they would plan a 500 or 600-mile trip. On arrival at the cotton fields, where primitive camps had been set up to house the cotton pickers, Fiona and Lois would establish their own little camp, and start treating the sick. Many of the Indians suffered from TB. The two nurses would start them on courses of treatment, and try to persuade them to return with them to the hospital at Juarez to continue the cure. Many of the children

had dreadful diarrhoea—their mothers did not
realize that the filthy water the children drank was
nearly always fouled by animals and people, and
should always be boiled. Most people suffered from
malnutrition—they did not have enough to eat and
the food seldom contained enough vitamins for
health. Fiona and Lois gave out vitamin tablets and
milk powder, and showed mothers how to feed their
hungry babies on goat's milk to help make them
strong. In the evenings Lois and Fiona would have
a sing-song, and read to the Indians from the Bible,
telling them the simple stories with the aid of
pictures, and teaching them how to pray.

On the way home from the cotton fields they
would stop their jeep in various villages and hold a
proper clinic; blowing the jeep's hooter when they
were ready to attend to patients. They kept a careful
record of vaccinations too. In England a baby is
vaccinated when it is a few months old, so that a
child is in no danger of catching smallpox. But the

children whom Fiona and Lois worked among had never been vaccinated and many of them died of the dreadful disease.

The old jeep owned by SAMS had to undergo some rough treatment travelling on the so-called roads around the Indian villages. It had huge tyres, like tractor tyres, and these cost £20 each to replace. A set of new tyres only lasted a year at the most, as the roads were very sandy and full of big holes. Thorns from the cactus, often six to eight inches long, played havoc with the tyres too, and tree stumps and fallen wood—half buried in the sandy surface—were an added danger. Sometimes the heat was so intense that the tyres would burst, and when a tyre was taken in for repairs the mechanic would sometimes find as many as fourteen small cuts and holes that needed mending.

One day, when they were returning from a 600 mile trip to the outlying cotton fields, the old jeep broke down. In spite of everyone's efforts nothing could be done to repair it. The jeep was a complete write-off.

'What are we going to do without transport?' Fiona said, when they were back at the Mission. She was voicing the thought that was uppermost in all their minds.

'We shall have to pray about it', Pat said quietly.

Lois had gone to the city to do some shopping and pick up some medicines. She decided to call in on the Field Superintendent, Bill, who had a visitor with him.

'This is a representative from OXFAM, Lois', Bill said. 'He would like to be shown round the area and told about the work that we're trying to do here'.

The Oxfam representative was interested in everything he saw, and finally turned to Lois and said, 'What would you say is your greatest need of the moment?'

Lois didn't hesitate. 'A jeep', she said simply. 'Ours has just broken down, and by the look of it will be completely useless'.

'I'll see what I can do', the man promised.

On his return to Oxfam HQ, he put in an official request and by August the money arrived for the SAMS missionaries to purchase a super new Ford truck!

It was a very exciting moment and a wonderful answer to the missionaries' prayer.

Fiona's life began to fall neatly into two parts. The times when she was living at home in Juarez in the little mud and brick house with Lois and Sylvia, who had come to join them as a teacher. They visited the local people and helped them when and where they could, other times they went on the more exciting missionary journeys out to distant villages.

Mind you, even life in their little brick house wasn't always without incident! One day when Fiona was passing from the bedroom to the sitting-room she saw something move in her bedroom. She stood against the wall and watched with horror as a rattlesnake slid along the hall and through the sitting-room door. Finally it came to rest curled up on the bookcase.

'Go and get Don Alfredo from next door', Fiona called quietly to Lois. 'There's a nasty big rattle-snake asleep on our bookcase'.

Don Alfredo came and looked at the snake with interest, but he didn't offer to touch it.

'Well, aren't you going to do something?' Fiona demanded.

'I don't know what to do', Alfredo admitted. 'I'll call the man over the fence. He catches them with a kind of lasso'.

Fiona waited anxiously, hoping the snake wouldn't decide to go on another tour of inspection.

Within a few moments the man and a young boy came in, carrying a tin can and a piece of string.

Fiona didn't feel much confidence in them until the man made a neat loop in the string, slipped it adroitly round the snake's neck, and whipped it into the can.

'You send it to Buenos Aires', he said, offering Fiona the closed can.

'What for?' Fiona wanted to know, taking the tin gingerly.

'They use it for making snake serum to treat snake-bite', Lois explained. 'They send us in return a supply of snake serum and another empty can'.

'Wasn't I brave?' Fiona enquired of Lois when the incident was over, and the girls were making themselves a cup of tea.

'Very brave', Lois said, 'I was really proud of you. You must be the strong silent type!'

She was to change her mind a couple of days later when she came running into the kitchen to find a screaming Fiona standing on the kitchen table, skirts held tightly round her and nodding towards the bathroom.

'Whatever is the matter?' she asked her terrified friend.

'A mouse!' Fiona shrieked. 'He ran into the bathroom!'

Work in Juarez is still going on. Fiona is now in charge of the nursing, and Barbara—a teacher—is responsible for the educational work. David and Charles are the pastors working with the churches, and Maurice teaches the people to grow better crops, and takes charge of some of the industries that are being formed to help the Indians earn some money, so that they can have an improved standard of living. Sylvia has returned to Rosario to complete her studies at the University.

There are now several small industries in Juarez. One of them is making posts for fencing. The trees are cut down and shaped into posts at forest camps, and then sold to big companies, who send their lorries to collect them from all over the country.

Tomato growing is also becoming quite a profitable industry, and the Indians are beginning to sell their wood-carvings and hand-woven articles. SAMS missionaries help and encourage, and find markets for the things the Indians can produce.

Oxfam have just ordered 50,000 wooden egg cups so if you see some in your local OXFAM shop they may have been made in Juarez by families who are being treated when they are ill by Fiona!

'We want to set up a main health centre in Juarez and put a nursing auxiliary in charge', Fiona told me. 'Then, when things are working smoothly, I will move on to four other key areas where I will hope to do the same thing. The centres will be staffed by trained Indian nursing auxiliaries. When all the centres have been opened I will travel round among them, helping with problems of sickness that are too complicated for the nursing auxiliary to cope with. We will teach the people the way to live healthy lives and concentrate on trying to prevent illnesses wherever possible. The health centres will work with the local state hospital—not apart from it—we do not have plans for setting-up separate mission hospitals of our own'.

'I used to think that missionary nurses always worked in mission hospitals', I said to Fiona the last time I was talking to her.

'Things are different now', she said. 'Missionary work has four parts—medical, educational, spiritual and social. The medical work looks after people's bodies, the educational looks after their minds, the spiritual after their spirits and the social side aims to help them to have better living conditions by providing useful ways of earning money. That is why we are trying to encourage the setting-up of industries. It's something the Indians cannot do on their own. If they earn more they will be able to feed their children better, and as the children become healthier they will be more capable of learning. We hope that in time we shall have happy, healthy Indian Christians leading full and useful lives to the glory of God'.

Fiona has just gone back from her first furlough home in England. She would like to feel that you are interested in her work, and are praying for her and the South American Indians she is trying to serve.

Cliff the Singer

Harry clung tightly to his mother's hand. The hot, dark bodies seemed to be pressing in on them and he felt frightened. His mother paused by a market stall to examine some fruit. Harry wished she would hurry so that they could get away from the unfriendly crowd. Suddenly a voice shouted at them. Harry couldn't tell where it came from, and he didn't understand the words, but his mother did.

'Why don't you go home to your own country, white woman?' The words were spat out in a bitter tone and everyone turned to stare at Harry's mother as she stood alone in the crowd, holding her little boy by the hand.

'Come on, let's go home, Harry', his mother said to his great relief, and the crowd drew back to let them through.

India was eager to be given the authority to rule itself, and hostile feeling was gradually building up against the British people who had been living and working there.

'Go home to your own country', Harry's mother had been told, but it was easier said than done. Harry's father had a good job in India, and the family had a comfortable home. It was not an easy decision to sell up and return to England where neither a job nor a home awaited them. But they decided to come home nevertheless.

In 1947, they booked passages on a ship to Tilbury, and arrived in England with only £5 in their pockets!

Seven-year-old Harry didn't enjoy the journey one bit. He was terribly seasick.

'I feel awful', he groaned, turning over on his side in his narrow bunk and wishing he were dead.

'Don't be such a baby', his father scolded, 'come up on deck and enjoy yourself. Your sister and I aren't wasting the voyage lying groaning in our bunks. You want some fresh air. You'll just feel worse if you lie there feeling sorry for yourself'.

Harry almost hated his father just then, but cheering himself with the thought that everyone would be sorry when he fell down and died in full view of everybody on the main deck, he crawled miserably out of his bunk and allowed his father to lead him up into the open air. Much to his surprise he soon felt much better and before long he was hungrily tucking into a good meal.

After the ship docked at Tilbury, Harry's family travelled to Carshalton in Surrey, where they were to stay with his grandmother until they found a home of their own.

Soon Harry started school. His skin was dark from years of exposure to the Indian sun, and the other children immediately pounced on him as someone who was different.

'Where you from, mate?' they asked him.

'From India', Harry replied shyly.

'Cor, did you live in a wigwam then? Where's your head-dress?'

Harry tried to explain that living in India didn't make you a Red Indian, but the children didn't want to listen.

'Red Indian Harry! Nigger! Nigger!' they yelled at him, so that Harry began to dread the sound of the bell that rang for 'break'.

But Harry didn't take the teasing meekly. Enraged, he would turn upon his tormentors and attack them violently with his fists, and in time they learned to respect him and left him in peace.

Life in Carshalton soon settled down to some kind of routine. Harry started to go to Sunday School with his three young cousins, whose family also lived with his grandmother, and sometimes Harry and his mother would go to church.

Harry's dad could never be persuaded to go.

'Church is not for people like me', he would say, if anyone tackled him about it.

It wasn't that Harry's father didn't believe in God. In fact, he often used to read stories from the Bible to Harry and his sister, but he didn't feel the Church was for ordinary working-class men and women, and so he preferred to stay away.

Harry didn't mind going to church, but he didn't find it very exciting, and it didn't really bother him if he went or not.

After 18 months, when Harry had at last got used to living in Carshalton, and had begun to feel reasonably happy in his new school, his father decided to move to Waltham Cross. Gran had been very good about having them to live with her, but they felt they couldn't impose on her any longer.

'My sister says she'll put us up', Harry's father said to his Mum. 'And I've been offered a job at Fergusons, the radio and TV factory. It's too good a chance to turn down and we stand a better chance in Waltham Cross of getting a house of our own'.

'Just as I've got used to this school, we've got to move', young Harry complained. 'And it's going to be pretty crowded living with Aunty if we're only going to have one room!'

'It's only for a while', Harry's Mum promised. 'Then we'll have a proper house of our own. And Kings Road School seems very nice'.

She was right. He liked his new school, and they did find a house. Or at least the Council Housing Officer found one for them, and Harry, his father and mother, his sister Donella, and the new baby, Joan, who had been born while they were living with their aunt, all moved into the new house.

It was red-brick, with two living-rooms and three bedrooms, and Harry's family were absolutely thrilled to be living in a home of their own once more.

Harry was doing quite well at school, and his parents were delighted when, soon after his 11th birthday, he was awarded a prize for being the school's top boy in class work.

'Well done, son', his father said. 'If you go on like this you'll pass your 11-plus exam and get to

Grammar School'.

But Harry's father was wrong. When the buff, foolscap envelope arrived through Harry's letter-box some months later, it contained the disappointing news that Harry was to continue his education at Cheshunt Secondary Modern School. To make matters worse, Harry found he wasn't even in the 'A' stream, and in those first weeks at his new school he felt a complete failure.

But the result of Harry's 11-plus exam didn't seem to reflect his ability very well, for, halfway through the first term, he was transferred to the 'A' stream where he felt much happier. He liked Cheshunt. He did well in English and Maths, and got on well with most of his teachers, particularly Mrs. Norris, the English teacher. He found he had a flair for acting too, and joined the school dramatic society. He also began to realise how much he enjoyed singing. When the dramatic society produced *Toad of Toad Hall*, Harry was given the part of Ratty. He had to sing a couple of songs, as well as acting, and they seemed to go down pretty well.

'Have you ever thought of taking up singing as a career, Harry?' Mrs. Norris asked him after the performance.

'Yes', Harry admitted, but he wasn't sure that Mrs. Norris' idea of a singing career was the same as his. Harry liked 'pop' music, and for a long time had secretly wondered if one day he could be a pop singer like Elvis Presley, and perhaps even have a group of his own.

Some weeks later the news got round the school that Bill Haley and the Comets—a very popular beat group—were coming to do a show at Edmonton, just a couple of miles away.

Harry and some of his friends decided to go.

'What will we do about school?' Harry wanted to know. 'They'll start queueing for tickets early in the morning. We won't stand a chance if we don't get there first thing'.

'We'll have to miss school' they all decided, and the next morning they got up before six o'clock and arrived at the theatre where the Comets were appearing. But there was already a queue, and in the end they didn't get their tickets until half-past eleven.

'By the time we've had something to eat, it won't be worth going back to school', was the general feeling, so they went back to Harry's house for a snack lunch.

'If we go back this afternoon they'll want to know where we've been', someone suggested, as they sat around and munched sandwiches. 'Why don't we take the afternoon off as well? We're going to get into a row anyway, so it might just as well be a good one'.

Everyone agreed. Their minds were full of the show that night, and mere school just didn't seem important.

Afterwards they all decided that it had been well worth it. And it was during the show, as Harry found himself caught up in the rhythm and excitement of the music, that he knew what he wanted to do more than anything else in the world. He wanted to sing, and perhaps play as well, with a beat group. Nothing else would satisfy him.

Next morning Harry and his friends came down to earth. They were sent for by the headmaster.

'You are all prefects', he said coldly. 'And as such I expect your behaviour to be above reproach. Playing truant from school, whatever the circumstances, is a serious breach of discipline. You leave me no alternative but to remove your prefects badges, together with your authority'.

'I don't think that's fair', Harry dared to protest. 'I bet it's only because we stayed away from school to get tickets for a beat concert. If we'd been to the Bolshoi Ballet or something like that, you'd have given us a pat on the back'.

But the headmaster was in no mood for argument, and when the boys left his study their prefects badges lay on his desk.

From then onwards Harry was determined to become a pop singer. He was prepared to start modestly, and to work tirelessly, so long as some day, somewhere, he could reach the top. The first group he belonged to was called the Quintones. It consisted of three girls and two boys, and they became quite popular at school concerts and other local events. When that folded up, Harry moved on to the Dick Teague Skiffle group, where he sang the solos. He also learned to play the guitar. It was an old one that had cost just over £5 several years before, and after three weeks' regular practice in the sitting-room at home, Harry could pick out tunes in three different keys. It was a beginning!

The skiffle group played at weddings, children's parties, a twenty-first birthday, badminton club suppers, and the like—which was quite an improvement on the Quintones' school concerts! Harry felt he was on the second rung of the ladder to fame, but there was one snag. Singing and playing with a skiffle group might be fun but it certainly didn't bring in enough money to take the place of a regular job.

'You'd better come and work at Fergusons with me', Harry's father said to him one day. 'There's no knowing if you will ever be able to make a career from singing. We think you're quite good—but there's a lot of competition you know. Very few groups ever seem to reach the top'.

Harry was forced to agree. He left school and started work as a clerk in the radio factory, limiting his pop singing and playing to the evenings and weekends.

But it wasn't long before Harry's ambitions made him restless again.

'I'm a bit fed up with the skiffle group', he confided to Terry the drummer, who was one of his oldest friends. 'I'm not sold on skiffle anyway. I'd like to form my own group and do more "rock and roll" stuff'.

To his delight Terry agreed with him, and so the soloist and the drummer parted company with Dick and his friends, and after enrolling another boy called Norman as rhythm guitarist they formed their own group which they called 'The Drifters', and got down to some serious practice in Harry's front room. But that led to some trouble!

Unfortunately for Harry and his friends not everyone on their housing estate enjoyed beat music, and it wasn't long before someone complained. An official from the town hall came to call. He proved surprisingly sympathetic.

'I can't ignore the complaint', he pointed out, 'but I'm reluctant to forbid you to practice altogether. Supposing you keep the windows and doors closed and pack up at ten o'clock? That will keep the noise down a bit and also mean you aren't disturbing people until the early hours of the morning'.

Harry and his friends gratefully agreed. It was hard on Harry's family who, night after night, had to endure a sealed house that was ringing with sound, but they never complained.

And then, one day, when the group had been functioning for some time, the Drifters got their first taste of success. They were invited to appear at a ballroom in Derby. The payment wasn't very wonderful—in fact, when they had time to work it out afterwards, it just about covered the group's return rail fares, but it was the honour that counted. The only thing that the manager didn't like about the group was their soloist's name.

'Harry and the Drifters', he said thoughtfully. 'It

isn't going to look very good on the advertising bill'.

Harry had never thought very much about his name before. *Harry* did not particularly appeal to him, but he was proud of his family surname and somehow wasn't very keen on the idea of changing it. However, he could see the manager's point. He and his friends sat down with the manager to think it out. In the end it was unanimously decided that from then on Harry should be known as *Cliff*, and 'Cliff and the Drifters' prepared to make their first public appearance.

The change of name seemed to bring success with it. 'Cliff and the Drifters' were kept busy with evening and weekend engagements, and then in 1958, when Cliff was just 18, he had a wonderful opportunity. An agent got in touch with him and offered him a four weeks' booking at Butlin's Holiday Camp at Clacton.

'I've managed to get a booking for you', the agent said. 'If I were you I should fix things up right away'.

'What do you mean, "me"?' Cliff wanted to know. 'What about the group?'

'I'm sorry', the agent said. 'They only want you as soloist. You'll be silly to turn down such a chance'.

It was a great temptation, but Cliff was determined to be loyal to his friends.

'Unless you book the group, you don't get me', he said. 'I won't be half as good without them. We're used to working together'.

In the end Butlin's gave in and agreed to sign on the whole group. Cliff was delighted. He gave in his notice to Fergusons, and went off to the seaside to enjoy his first long engagement as a singer. After that things moved quickly. The Drifters made their first record and Cliff was also invited to appear in a TV pop show called 'Oh Boy'. He went on a fortnight's stage tour too, and was offered a part in a film called 'Serious Charge'.

It was all very exciting. People were anxious to interview him and record his opinions in papers and magazines. They wanted to know the things he liked to eat, the clothes he would choose and the kind of girl he wanted to marry.

They also wanted to know what he thought about God.

'There's one thing I feel very strongly about', he said in 1960, 'and that's religion. One's own religion —whatever else becomes public one's own belief should be private'.

'It's so important to have faith in something, and it's equally important no one ever laughs at you for the beliefs you hold', Cliff said on another occasion. 'I don't care if a person is Church of England, Jewish, or Buddhist, as long as he believes in something and is a decent person'.

One day Cliff was to change his mind about keeping his belief private, and he was to learn that belief in a vague 'something' wasn't enough. But he didn't know that at the time.

As the months went by Cliff became more and more popular, and his records topped the Top Twenty charts for 50 of the 52 weeks in 1961. He was awarded two Golden Discs for records selling over a million copies, and he made three films and sixteen records.

His family shared in his success. In 1959 he bought his parents a lovely house in Winchmore Hill, and in 1960 his father gave up his own job to help Cliff with the business and planning side of his career. Cliff was very fond of his family and that is why, in May 1961, when his father died in hospital of a heart condition, Cliff felt that things would never be quite the same again.

Soon afterwards Cliff went to Australia on a concert tour. He was still missing his father very much. One night he was talking to his friend Brian, who was a member of the Shadows, as the group was now called.

'I miss Dad a lot', Cliff said. 'Do you think there is any way of getting in touch with people after they are dead? If I thought there was, I should feel inclined to try'.

'Do you really want my opinion?' Brian asked.

'Of course I do', Cliff said.

'Then I'm dead against it', Brian said firmly.

'But why?' Cliff wanted to know.

'Haven't you ever read what the Bible says about it?' Brian asked.

Cliff was amazed. He hadn't really thought that the Bible had anything at all to say that might be useful in up-to-date situations, and he was amazed that his friend apparently thought it worth considering. Brian showed him several passages that warned against trying to get in touch with the spirits of people who have died, and Cliff was quite impressed. He started to read the Bible on his own.

Slowly he began to look at things in a different way. He realized that there was more to life than he had thought. Although success and money and popularity were all quite fun to possess, he had known for quite a long time that they didn't really give one any real satisfaction. It was rather like our ordinary physical appetite. You could eat a good meal but in a few hours' time you would be hungry again. Success didn't satisfy one for long, and Cliff sometimes longed for the kind of satisfaction that would really last.

He was also surprised to find that another of his close friends, Hank, was thinking about God as well, and they often discussed and argued about the Bible and the amazing things it had to say. Both of

them stopped swearing at this time, and they were
very keen to find out what God, and the Bible, and
going to church, had to do with living your everyday
life.

In 1964 Cliff went to see his old English teacher,
Mrs. Norris. He had always kept in touch with her
and he often found time to visit her.

'I can't sort out this business of religion', Cliff
confessed. 'So many people have so many different
views, and at times even the Bible seems to con-
tradict itself. I wish I knew the right answers to
some of the questions I want to ask'.

'I don't know that I have the answers you want',
Mrs. Norris said. 'But I think I know someone who
might. There's a young RI teacher at school whom
I'd like you to meet. He's the very person you
should talk to'.

Cliff was interested, and Mrs. Norris agreed to
arrange a meeting at his house. In the end three
people turned up: Mrs. Norris, Bill (the school
teacher), and Bill's friend, Graham.

Cliff found Bill and Graham very easy to talk to,
and he absolutely bombarded them with questions.
He liked them as people too, and he approved of the
way they looked for the answers to his questions in
the Bible, and didn't just try to give him their own
ideas.

A few weeks later Mrs. Norris invited Cliff to a
party and there he met Bill again.

'What do you do with yourself in your spare
time?' Cliff asked Bill, as they helped themselves to

some snacks from the tempting selection Mrs. Norris had provided. 'I know you teach RI in school, but you must have some free time in the evenings and at weekends'.

'I'm a Crusader leader', Bill told him. 'And believe you me, that doesn't leave you much spare time for anything else'.

'Sounds like banners and armour and horses', Cliff joked, 'as far as I can remember from the history books!'

'Modern Crusaders isn't quite like that', Bill said with a laugh. 'It's an organization of Bible Classes for young people throughout the country. We have a class on Sundays for Bible teaching, and leisure time activities during the week. We run outings and camps too, and cruises on the Broads during the summer'.

'Sounds interesting', Cliff commented.

'It is', Bill agreed. 'And very worthwhile, although it's hard work as well. Why don't you come along one Sunday and see what it's all about? We have about sixty boys in our class—all ages from eight to eighteen. We're always pleased to have visitors'.

Cliff was intrigued to be invited as an ordinary 'visitor' and not as a celebrity. He was beginning to get a bit tired of people who were only interested in him as a 'star' and not as an ordinary person.

He decided to accept Bill's invitation. He went along to a Sunday Crusader class and sat at the back and watched and listened, and came away feeling very impressed.

He was now reading the Bible regularly and one evening, when he'd been talking for a long time with a small group of people about Christianity, he asked the question that was to change his life.

'If I want to be a real Christian, exactly what do I have to do?'

'Admit and confess your sins', came the reply. 'Believe that Jesus Christ died so that you could be forgiven, and put your whole trust in Him'. Cliff became very thoughtful, and soon after that the gathering broke up. As people were leaving Cliff said quietly to Bill,

'I'm on my way in'.

During the autumn of 1965 Cliff became a changed person. His vague dissatisfaction with life completely disappeared, and he began to talk quite freely about his new found faith and the Christian activities in which he quickly became involved. He still enjoyed show business, but it became plain that his life was now directed by a far more powerful force than a personal desire for success.

'I've been in this game so long now that I've achieved most of the things I set myself to do', he told an interviewer for a women's magazine. 'Now I must find something else to aim at. I want to do something worthwhile with my life'.

Slowly Cliff began to wonder if God was asking him to give up the world of pop singing and do another job for Him, which might prove to be more satisfying and valuable. Many of his new Christian friends were teachers. Cliff began to wonder if God was calling him to be a teacher too. He knew that it would need a lot of thought and prayer before he could be quite sure about it.

Meanwhile the Billy Graham Evangelistic Association, who were planning a big Crusade in London, wrote to Cliff.

The letter said something like this:

'Dear Cliff,

I've heard that you are a Christian and are involved in youth work. Would you be prepared to come on the platform at one of our rallies at Earls Court? We thought it would be a help to many young people if you would be prepared to sing and give a few words of testimony'.

Cliff had mixed feelings about the whole affair. Large audiences had never worried him very much before, but this would be different. He would be singing—not for his own personal triumph—but as an ambassador of Jesus Christ. He would also be burning his boats behind him. Once he had made this personal and public declaration of his faith there would be no turning back. He would be committed for life.

On the other hand he was being offered a wonderful opportunity of serving the Master under whose colours he had now enlisted. The song he was to sing was called, 'It is no secret'. Was he prepared to make his own personal secret known to the world—that he, Cliff, was now a Christian and a servant of the Lord Jesus Christ?

'It took me quite a long time to pluck up enough courage', Cliff confessed. 'But in the end I managed it'.

On the night of Thursday, June 16th, 1966, Cliff found himself on the platform at Earls Court.

'I was absolutely terrified', he has told people since. 'I now know what the word "petrified" really means. It means "turned to stone", and that's just how I felt! I held on to the lectern with both hands, so tightly that when I tried to take my hands away afterwards they felt as if they were just frozen in that position for good! You see, I knew that there could be no turning back for me. If ever I did it would be like giving a black mark to all I claimed to stand for'.

At this time Cliff made up his mind that he wanted to be confirmed. He had been baptized as a baby, but now that he had become a convinced Christian, he felt he wanted to commit himself publicly to Jesus Christ, so he started to attend confirmation classes. They lasted for several months and at last on December 6th, 1966, Cliff knelt beside a young solicitor's clerk in his own church in Finchley and heard the Bishop say these words as he laid his hands on Cliff's head.

'Defend, O Lord, this thy child Cliff with thy heavenly grace that he may continue thine for ever; and daily increase in thy Holy Spirit more and more until he come unto thine everlasting kingdom. Amen'.

Cliff, the singer, the entertainer, the film star, the Golden Disc holder, the TV personality, the idol of tens of thousands of teenagers, had publicly acknowledged himself to be:

Cliff—the servant of the Lord Jesus Christ.

Now that Cliff had publicly identified himself with Christianity, invitations from Christian organizations all over the country began to flow in at such a rate that at last his friend Bill offered to deal with them. Cliff gratefully accepted. He was still greatly in demand as an entertainer, of course, and it was sometimes difficult to fit everything in. He had become a leader of the Finchley Crusader class and gave up quite a lot of his time to camps and rallies.

Cliff was still thinking of giving up his career as a singer and becoming a teacher. He had an interview for a training college and took a General Certificate of Education exam.

'Am I prepared to give it all up? That's what I have to ask myself', Cliff wondered. 'I've got opportunities in films on televison, and on the stage.

I've got everything I've always wanted and worked for. And if God is asking me to give it up and do another kind of job for Him, I've got to be prepared to do it'.

Cliff must have fought a long uphill battle over the whole question, but at last he was ready to face up to the answer.

'Yes, I am prepared. If this is what God wants me to do, I will give up show business altogether and become a teacher'.

That's what Cliff decided in 1967.

But once he had made the decision a very strange thing happened. Cliff suddenly became convinced that he could serve God much more effectively as a singer than as a teacher. TV opportunities started to open out to him and he was asked to appear in a Christian film, 'Two a Penny'. He began to realize very clearly just how effectively the Christian message could be got over in song. Young people from all over the country flocked to Christian meetings and rallies to hear Cliff tell them of his new found faith in Jesus Christ, and to listen to him singing Gospel songs and playing his guitar.

'Just because many of my closest Christian friends are teachers, that doesn't necessarily mean that God wants me to be a teacher as well', he realized. 'He gave me my voice in the first place, so it's pretty clear that He intends me to use it in His name'.

Being a singer who is also a convinced Christian gives Cliff wonderful opportunities for witnessing to his faith.

Show business people often ask him, 'Hey, Cliff, what's this Christianity all about?'

Cliff makes sure his TV shows are all good clean fun too. He's not prepared to take part in anything that might bring dishonour to his Master's name. He was invited to do a series of six programmes on Sunday evenings. They were called 'Sing a New Song', and showed how Christian music could be lively and attractive.

Cliff is able to use his money for God as well. He has just bought a lovely house in the country which is being run as a Christian Arts Centre, and where people who need time to think about the more important things in life can have a time and a place to do so. Cliff still thoroughly enjoys his musical shows both on stage and television, but nothing gives him greater satisfaction than an opportunity to demonstrate his very real and living faith.

'If you take rallies and meetings and put them alongside my concerts they completely overshadow my secular work', he says.

'I find it far more satisfying to do a meeting than a concert because I get the chance to use my profession, which is singing and talking and being able to communicate, and yet I feel I've done something really worthwhile—something that needs to be done.

'Shows can be a bit dangerous really because when you have a successful show you can't help feeling it's a personal achievement, and you have to remind yourself that whatever gifts you have, they are God's gifts anyway. You need to make an attempt to remain humble about it in front of God. Whereas when you do a Christian meeting, and it's successful, you know full well that it's nothing to do with you, and you are just an instrument'.

Cliff hasn't at the moment got any ideas about giving up his profession in order to serve God in other ways.

'If God plans that this should happen', he says, 'then I'm sure He'll let me know'.

There are many different ways of serving God and passing on the good news about Jesus Christ to other people, and Cliff has certainly discovered one of them.

June the Doctor

Hello everybody,

This is Doctor June speaking to you by means of a tape recorder from our mission hospital in Thailand, which, as you probably know, is a country to the south of China shaped something like an elephant's head. I understand you want to know how I came to be a missionary doctor, and how I knew that God was calling me to work for Him out here.

Well, I suppose it started when I was about six years old! I'll try and tell you all about it. My father was a doctor and we lived in Hastings. I was the youngest in our family and I had three sisters and two brothers, and all of them were very much older than I was. My mother and father were quite old by the time I was born and my brothers and sisters were nearly grown up. At least they seemed grown up to me, and they certainly hadn't got much time for a rather spoiled small sister who was always getting under their feet and pestering them to play games with her!

One day my mother had an idea.

'I'm going to see if June can go to school' she said.

'But she's only three years old', my father protested. 'They surely won't take her at school until she is five at least'.

'I'm going to try', my mother said. 'She'd be much happier at school than moping about at home with nothing to do. And the girls could take her and bring her home again'.

My mother got her way, and I started school. I liked school and I soon learned to read and write. I enjoyed having plenty of friends to play with, and I liked the headmistress of our school very much. She was an artist as well as a teacher, and although I was too little to realize it at the time, I know now that she was also a Christian. She loved the Bible very much, and she taught us to love it too. She often read us stories from it, and showed us pictures, and taught us about the Lord Jesus and the good things that He did when He lived on earth.

One day, when I had been at school for about three years, we had a Scripture lesson that I was to remember for the rest of my life. Our teacher told us that if we wanted to lead really happy and satisfying lives, we had got to be quite sure that we were doing the will of God, and were working in the job He had chosen for us. I thought about what the teacher had said, and later when we were out in the playground I said to a group of my friends,

'I'm not going to do the will of God. I'm going to be a doctor!'

I didn't know then that one day God would bring these two things together, and although I would be a doctor I would also be doing God's will!

When I was about eight my grandparents came to live with us. I liked Granny and Granpa very much but I did wish that I had someone of my own age to play with. My older brothers and sisters teased me, and Granny and Granpa spoiled me, and the maid who helped my mother run the house did whatever I asked her to, but they all seemed so *old* and never wanted to play leap-frog in the garden or squash into dark cupboards for a game of hide and seek. Sometimes I felt very lonely and bored, and that is why I was absolutely delighted when Mother and Dad decided to send me to boarding school.

The school was in the country near Brighton. It was quite a small school. There were only about 50 pupils and only 30 of those 'boarded in', so it didn't take long to get to know everyone.

I soon settled down and was very happy during term time, but in the holidays I was still lonely. I can remember one family holiday when this was especially so. We had gone to Swanage with a family of cousins. They were all the same age as my brothers and sisters and so, of course, they all went off together and didn't want a lonely 12-year-old tagging along at their heels. I was looking around the shops in the town with my parents when a rather pretty girl in her late teens stopped to talk to me.

'Are you on holiday here?' she asked.

'Yes', I said shyly, surprised that someone I didn't know should notice me.

'I'm from a Children's Holiday Mission', she said. 'We hold meetings for boys and girls on the beach each day. Perhaps you've seen our banner?

Why don't you come along and join us. We play
games in the mornings, and then we sing choruses
and tell stories from the Bible. Sometimes we all go
swimming or have sand castle competitions, or play
cricket on the beach as well'.

'I'll think about it', I said, and then my mother
came up and it was time to go.

I did think about it. I thought about it for two
days, and on the third day I decided to go along
and try it. After all, anything would be better than
always playing by myself.

There were a lot of boys and girls gathered round
the big banner on the beach and they seemed to be
enjoying themselves. The trouble was that most of
them seemed to know one another, and no one
noticed when I came up and stood about near the
edge of the crowd. They were singing choruses, but
I didn't know any of the tunes or the words, and
there didn't seem to be quite enough books to go
round. I stood there, first on one foot and then on
the other, hoping that someone would notice me
and help me to feel one of the crowd, but nobody
did. After the singing we had a Bible story, and as
I turned to go away, one of the leaders gave me a
coloured card with a text on it. I put it in the
nearest litter basket on my way back across the
beach, and vowed that I would never go to the
meeting again.

It was a pity because I think if some of the boys
and girls had realized how lonely I was, they would
have made an effort to be friendly, and then perhaps

I would have learned about being a Christian when I was 12 instead of waiting for another five years.

After the holidays I went back to school again and I stayed at the school until I was 15, when I passed my School Certificate with flying colours. There was only one problem.

I had, by this time, quite definitely made up my mind that I wanted to be a doctor. My father was a doctor, and my eldest sister was training to be a doctor, and I wanted to be a doctor as well. Although I had done well at school I had not studied many Science subjects—only Botany. If I was going to go to Medical School when I was 17 I would have to take Physics, Chemistry and Biology, and I would have to master them in double quick time.

When my father was a boy he had been to school at Clifton, in Bristol. Now he decided to send me there too. I would join the sixth form and would have to work very hard at my Science subjects if I was to be able to enter medical school in two years' time. The war was now on and Bristol was being badly bombed. The boarding pupils at Clifton were moved outside the city to a stately home and we came into school each day by bus. The boarding house was a lovely place to live. It had big grounds and was set in the middle of the most beautiful countryside, and it was there that I first began to be interested in bird life, and to learn about plants and flowers. My school work didn't go too well.

'June is very much below standard', the head-mistress warned my father at one rather stormy interview. 'Her Science subjects are well below average for her age, and at times I think she finds it hard to keep up'.

'June didn't study Chemistry, Physics or Biology at all at her last school', my father defended me. 'She is an intelligent girl and is prepared to work. I shall be glad if you will arrange special coaching'.

The special coaching did the trick, and in 1942, with my school exams safely behind me, I entered Bristol University to read Medicine.

At first I had thought of going to the London School of Medicine for Women, at the Royal Free Hospital, but my father advised me against it. My eldest sister had trained there and had been the Gold Medallist of her year.

'Some of the same professors will be there', my father warned. 'You will feel you are always having to compete with your sister's record. You both look rather alike too. It will be much better for you to train at a completely different place where you will be assessed on your own merits'. I am glad I listened to his advice.

On my first day at the university I made two friends. One of them was called Joy. She was going to train to become a doctor as well. The other girl was called Nancy, and she was reading French. That evening, we were sitting having coffee in the Common Room when suddenly Joy leapt out of her seat and came and peered at a small badge on the lapel of Nancy's jacket.

'You're a Crusader!' she cried in delight. 'And so am I!' I didn't really know what there was to get so excited about, but they started to chatter nineteen to the dozen, and behaved as if they had known each other for years.

I understand now the way they felt. It's always exciting to discover another Christian when you move to a new place or job. You feel a close bond with them straight away, because you know that your Lord is their Lord as well.

Joy and Nancy and I became great friends. In fact really there were six of us in our special 'group'. Two of us were Christians—that was Joy and Nancy —two of us were Roman Catholics, one of us hadn't got any kind of faith at all, and then there was me. I didn't really know where I fitted in, and even Joy and Nancy weren't sure! I was quite happy to go with them to the Christian Union meetings and the squashes that were organized for all the new students. A squash is a friendly meeting held in a home or a student's room. Lots of people 'squash in' and coffee is provided while you sit around and chat. Perhaps somebody will play the piano or a guitar, and start people singing, and the evening ends with a few verses being read from the Bible, and a short talk about being a Christian and what it means. I even agreed to go to a prayer meeting, although that gave me a bit of a shock. I'd never met such a thing before! A roomful of people gathered together and praying to God in their own words, without even using a prayer book! I really felt quite out of my depth.

You know, some people can think back to a particular day, or even hour, when they became a Christian. With me it was nothing as definite as that. I never made a special black and white resolution, and there wasn't one definite moment of decision for me, but gradually, over those first months at university, through attending Bible studies and meetings, and talking long into the night with Joy and Nancy, I slowly but surely realized that I needed a Saviour, and took the Lord Jesus Christ for my Master and Lord.

During the Christmas vacation I knew that I had become a different person. I now read my Bible regularly and was learning how to pray. I wanted to go to church and worship with other Christian people, and I began to realize that perhaps God would want to have a say in my career.

Of course the way wasn't always smooth and easy. I had boy friend trouble for one thing.

I had arranged to go to a university dance with

my boy friend, and he let me down at the last minute. It was a tremendous blow, but, sitting in my room crying about it, I had time to think.

I knew that I was now a Christian, and I also knew that my boy friend wasn't. If things got serious between us I could see it would never work out. We would always be pulling in different directions. Perhaps it was as well that I had realized this before I got too deeply involved. I went down on my knees that night and put my whole life under God's control. I can even remember the date. It was the 15th of March. I think that was the moment that God's Holy Spirit really took control of my life, and from that time onwards I began to feel, quite clearly, that God wanted me to serve Him as a doctor on the mission field somewhere overseas.

At first I didn't know where He wanted me to go. I had read a lot about the China Inland Mission and about its great founder, Hudson Taylor. In fact I had failed one set of medical examinations because

I read both volumes of the story of his life instead of revising during the summer vac!

'Perhaps God wants me to go to China', I thought.

In 1949, when I was 24, I took my final exams and became a qualified doctor. I was still thinking about going to China, so I chose my first jobs with that thought in mind. First I became a Surgical and Casualty Officer, then I worked for 18 months at the Bethnal Green Medical Mission, where I learned to work as part of a team. After that I learned more about women's illnesses and the delivery of babies, realizing that I ought to have as wide an experience of medicine as possible before applying for a job on the mission field overseas.

But alas, the doors into China were closing. The Communists were taking over and the China Inland Mission was having to pull out. I could see that God must have other plans for me.

I wrote to several missionary societies and had flatteringly keen replies back from most of them. Doctors were needed everywhere. I needn't be afraid of not getting a job. But I didn't want just *any* job with *any* missionary society. If I was to give up my life to working for God overseas I wanted to be absolutely sure that I was doing the one special job, in the one special place, that He intended for me.

Although I had been in touch with them several times I decided to write to the China Inland Mission once again.

'What are your future plans?' I asked. 'Will you be working somewhere else as a Mission now that the doors of China are closed to you ?'

The CIM wrote back.

'We have sent out a team to see where the greatest need exists', the letter said. 'After prayerful consideration of their reports we have decided that we shall set our sights on Southern Asia and that one of the areas in greatest medical and spiritual need is Central Thailand. We shall be changing the name of our Society to the Overseas Missionary Fellowship, and will pursue our normal policy of organizing medical and evangelistic work hand in hand.

'We shall be considering new candidates in the autumn and enclose application forms in case you are interested.'

I was interested, and with a strong assurance from the Lord that I was doing the right thing, I filled in the forms and sent them off.

Some months later, following several interviews, I was accepted by OMF and after a year's training, a term of which took place at the London Bible College, I set out for Thailand.

The first 18 months I spent in language study. Thai is a difficult language and even now I do not speak it really fluently, although I can understand everything I need to know, and can prepare a simple message or Bible study and chat to my patients about their illnesses.

Language study is always a difficult and trying time for a missionary, and I was glad when at last I moved out to a village clinic and could spend half my time at medical work and the other half con-

tinuing my studies of the language. The clinics
where we worked were just rough wooden shelters,
with a sloping roof made of corrugated tin. Inside
were some benches and chairs, a desk and lots of
pictures and bright posters on the walls; this was
where the patients waited. We doctors had a small
room partitioned off from the rest of the building
where we could see our patients one at a time.

For a year I worked with another doctor and then
I was put in full charge of a clinic of my own. We
had no proper hospital at that time, and so very sick
people, who needed operations, had to be sent by
boat down the river to Bangkok. This took about
six hours and wasn't a pleasant experience for
someone who was very ill.

All this time people all over the world who sup-
ported the Overseas Missionary Fellowship had
been praying that it would be possible to open a
Christian hospital in Central Thailand, and one day
news came through that at last God was answering
their prayers. We had been officially invited by the
District and Education Officers to build our first
hospital in Manoram, and a suitable piece of land
had been donated by a local landowner. You can
imagine how excited we all were when in August
1956 the original wooden hospital was opened.

I had begun to be specially interested in the
treatment of leprosy. You will remember that
people suffered from this terrible disease in the time
of Jesus, and they had to leave their work and their
homes and their families, and go off and live by

themselves so that other people would not catch it. There was a lot of leprosy in Thailand, and although the disease can now be cured quite easily with modern drugs and treatment, many of the Thai people had never had the chance to come to a hospital to be made well. If the disease is not treated, it causes terrible damage to the patient's limbs, and in time he may be unable to use his hands or his feet at all.

Part of our hospital work is to train the patients to do useful jobs, so that they may be able to earn their own living again.

Even before the new hospital was built, providing a wing where leprosy patients could be treated, we realized that a special doctor would be needed to supervise this work. The nurses looking after the clinics were women, and the doctor would work closely with them—therefore it would be better if the doctor were a woman. Also she would be travelling and spending nights away with the nurses, therefore it would be best if the doctor were unmarried. The doctor would visit the various leprosy clinics spread over a very large area. Later when the leprosy wing was built she would treat the patients there as well. Gradually I began to feel that God wanted me to do this job.

It was now 1959 and I was due to come home on furlough as I had been in Thailand for four years. A well known specialist who was an expert in the treatment of leprosy was due to visit Thailand, and so it was arranged that I should take my holiday in

England, and then return to Thailand in time to
have two months special training under him. And
that is how it worked out. I went all over Thailand
with the specialist and his wife, visiting leprosy
centres, and learning all I could about the methods
of treatment, and in 1960 I settled down in Manoram
in charge of my own leprosy department there.

I'm still at Manoram today, but things have
changed a lot during the last ten years. When I took
over we had about 15 clinics to visit, now we have

26. I used to travel for long distances on a bicycle
or motor-cycle. Now I have a smart Ford Escort
estate car. I used to pedal my way over tracks
through the fields, often falling off my bicycle into
the wet muddy rice fields. Now we have good new
roads. I used to stay in Thai homes, eating and
sleeping on the floor, and bathing in my sarong (the
dress Thai women wear) watched by 50 or 60
interested villagers; now I have a pleasant three-
roomed flat with a bathroom, overlooking the

hospital compound. Our first hospital buildings were made of wood, but in August 1969 a beautiful new concrete hospital was opened with air-conditioned operating theatres, light airy wards, up to date laboratories and treatment rooms.

The leprosy work is still my special care, but now we have the disease well under control. Wonderful modern drugs can treat and cure leprosy, and when the disease is caught in its early stages patients can often be treated in their homes. I don't have to spend all of my time in the leprosy department now, but can take my share of responsibility in the general hospital work.

I haven't told you much about the evangelistic work that goes on in and around the hospital, have I? The 'evangel' is the good news about Jesus Christ, and an evangelist is someone who passes this good news on to other people. We always take an evangelist with us when we visit the clinics, and while the nurses and I are treating the patients, the evangelist will talk to them about the Lord Jesus Christ, and tell them Bible stories, and sometimes give them booklets in the Thai language which tells them how they can become Christians and serve the Lord Jesus Christ.

We have two churches in the hospital compound. The one for 'well' people has its own building between the hospital and the village, and the church for leprosy patients meets underneath the rehabilitation centre which is built on stilts. Soon they hope to build a proper church as well. Both are run by a committee of church leaders with missionaries as advisors.

We have a lending library in the hospital too, where patients can borrow books that will help them to understand the Christian faith.

As our work at the hospital has grown, so the number of Christians has grown too. Ten to 15 years ago there was hardly a single Christian north of Bangkok. We would often visit villages to preach and give out tracts, where they had never even heard of the Lord Jesus Christ. Now there are little church groups scattered over the whole area and at least 500 to 600 Thai people are established Christians.

I love every moment of my work here, and I think that the Christian life is absolutely thrilling. I can't think how anyone, especially doctors, can possibly manage without the Lord Jesus Christ to guide them! I'm always asking Him for advice, and I'm always so grateful to have Him to turn to when I have to make a quick decision. My days are so busy and full that I can't begin to imagine what I would do without His help.

I know that being a doctor is the right job for me, and that working in Manoram hospital is the right place. Unless the Lord showed me very clearly that He wanted me elsewhere I wouldn't think of moving.

I often smile to think of that funny little six-year-old who said: 'I'm not going to do the will of God —I'm going to be a doctor!'

The tape on my tape recorder has nearly run out, but I think I've just got time to say 'Good-bye'. Will you think about me sometimes working in the Christian hospital at Manoram, and pray that my patients may not only get well again, and be helped to lead full and useful lives, but may also learn something about the love of the Lord Jesus Christ while I am looking after them?

With good wishes to you all,

Doctor June.

Jeanette the Captain

Nicolette and I are twins. We are both officers in the Salvation Army. We used to go to the Salvation Army Sunday School from the time that we were about five, and sometimes in the week we went to the Joy Hour, which was held after school on a piece of ground called 'The City Bank' when it was fine, and indoors if the weather was wet or cold. The Salvation Army Officers would play rounders and cricket with us, and then we would sing choruses and listen to a story from the Bible. One of the officers had an accordion, and he could play it very well. I often used to wonder how he could carry all the tunes in his head, because he never seemed to need any music.

Sometimes I got fed up with going to Sunday school and would threaten to leave.

'If you leave, you won't be able to go to the outing and the Christmas party!' Nicolette would warn me. 'And you'll lose your attendance prize!'

We looked forward to the outing and the party all the year, so when Nicolette reminded me about them, I decided to stay on after all.

We were both in the Singing Company too. That's what they called the children's choir. We used to sing at concerts, and sometimes during the morning or afternoon services. I liked to sing with the choir. It made me feel important.

I went to the Junior School quite near our home and then when I was eleven I moved up into the Senior School. I quite liked school, especially games and art. I wasn't bad at history and English either, but I hated maths. I couldn't bear being told off at school and sometimes I was quite rude when the teachers kept on at me. One teacher remarked on this in my school report. He wrote:

'Very aggressive when reprimanded', which is another way of saying, 'Gets mad when told off!'

My mother was simply furious when she read it, and told me I'd better learn to hold my tongue or I'd be finding myself in trouble!

When I was nearly fifteen I got a job. It wasn't a proper job, of course, because I was still at school. I only worked in the evenings and at week-ends. I was a kind of mother's help. A lady who lived near Cirencester had three children who were all very close together in age. I used to go round and give them their baths and put them to bed, and at week-ends I would take them for walks, and sometimes babysit so that their parents could go out. The children were called Bernard, Julie and Esther, and their father worked at the Admiralty. I think he was a naval captain. I liked helping with the children, and it was a good way of earning some pocket money too. I began to think that perhaps, when I left school, I'd like to take a job that had something to do with children, so that I could work with them all the time.

When I was fifteen I left school, and at the same time the naval captain decided to move to Barnet in Hertfordshire. One day the captain's wife had a talk with me.

'I know you are about to leave school, Jeanette', she said. 'And I've found it very useful to have you to help with the family. My husband and I will be moving away from Cirencester soon, and we'd like to take you with us. Do you think you would like to come?'

I was getting a bit fed up with Cirencester by that time and there wasn't much to do in the evenings, so I had a talk with my mother about the captain's wife's suggestion, and she said I could go if I wanted to. So within a few weeks I'd settled down in Barnet. Nicolette was working in Chelsea as an assistant nanny to quite a posh family, so we used to see quite a bit of each other on our days off. Nicolette had joined the Chelsea Salvation Army, but I didn't go to church at all at that time. The captain and his family never used to bother, and somehow I hadn't the courage to let them know that I thought God was a pretty important person, and one ought to go to church to worship Him. Actually, one night I did go to the Salvation Army hall in Barnet, and then, when I came out afterwards, I wondered what I was going to tell the captain and his wife. I knew they would ask me where I had been, and I was afraid they would laugh at me if I told them the truth. On the way home I slipped into a cinema and watched the tail-

end of a film. I thought I could say I had been to
the pictures and could back up the lie by telling
them a bit about the film. It's funny, you care such
a lot what people think when you're about sixteen.
Now I am older I don't bother nearly so much
about what other people think—I just do what I
think is right.

I've only told you about Nicolette and myself up
until now, but there are six children in my family.
I have an older sister called Anne and an older
brother called Nigel, and then there are Cherry and
Josephine—they are both younger than me.

When I'd been with the captain's family for about
a year my sister Anne got married, and Nicolette
and I went home to be bridesmaids. I remember it
was just before Christmas, and on the Sunday
evening after the wedding the Salvation Army were
putting on a Christmas play. Nicolette and I both
wanted to go and see it, but we didn't see how we
were going to manage it. We were due back in
London that night and the coach left at about seven
o'clock.

'Let's dawdle down to the coach station', I said
to Nicolette, 'and make sure we don't get there
until after the coach has left. Then we can go back
and tell Mum we've missed the coach with a
perfectly clear conscience'.

Nicolette wasn't sure it was a very honest plan,
but she wanted to see the play too, so that was what
we did.

Anyway, it was lucky in a way that we did miss

the coach, because some of the older children who had parts in the play hadn't returned from a school outing, and so the officer who was producing it was in quite a state. She asked Nicolette and me if we were prepared to 'stand in'. We were supposed to be shepherds, and we had about ten minutes to learn our parts! I forgot my words as soon as I came on the stage and saw all the people in the audience. I was frightened to death and I couldn't think of a word to say! Then I started to say someone else's words! I felt awful.

'Just a minute, folks, that was wrong!' I apologized to the audience, and then I darted off and had a quick look at the script. Everyone laughed of course, but at least when I came back I knew what to say!

When we were seventeen Nicky and I both came back to Cirencester. We had had enough of living away from home for a while. I got a job in the CWS Creamery just outside the town, and Nicky went to work at a laundry. It wasn't an ordinary laundry. It was one of those places that supplies clean towels to shops and offices, and the dirty towel rolls are replaced with clean ones each day.

The job at the Creamery was quite interesting. I had to feed lids into a container that tinned milk, and control the level of the milk as it was put into the tins. We didn't do the same job all the time so it wasn't as boring as it might have been. Sometimes I worked in the packing department, packing the tins into cardboard boxes, and sometimes I loaded tins on to the conveyor belt ready to be labelled.

In the evenings I went around with a group of friends. We spent most of our time in the local coffee bar. Everyone seemed to smoke so I started as well, just to show that I could keep up with the rest of the gang. None of us seemed to have much purpose in life. Most of the kids only wanted to have plenty of money so that they could have a good time. Nicky wasn't very keen on my kind of friends and never went with me to the coffee bar, even though I often tried to persuade her. She used to try and get me to come to the Salvation Army with her, but I had had enough of it for the time being. One Sunday she had a special 'go' at me.

'Why don't you come to the Army any more, Jeanette?' she asked. 'You always used to enjoy it. It's only that you've got out of the habit lately. Why don't you try to make a fresh start?'

'It's no good keeping on at me, Nicky', I said stubbornly, 'I don't want to go—and that's that'.

But one Sunday night I changed my mind. I went and sat at the back of the hall and hoped no one would notice me. I wasn't very impressed, but somehow the next week I went again, and this time I felt very uncomfortable. I knew that I was just wasting my life away, and I felt that I ought to do something about it. I knew what I ought to do, too, but I wasn't at all keen to do it.

On the third Sunday I told Nicky I was going to the Army on the Sunday night, so we sat together. I remember the Captain spoke on John 3.16, 'For God so loved the world, that He gave His only begotten Son, that whosoever believeth in Him should not perish, but have everlasting life'. Somehow it seemed as if the words hit home at me for the first time. 'For God so loved the world'—the world of people, and me in particular—that's what I felt God was saying to me.

After the talk we had a time of prayer. I knelt with my head in my hands feeling very miserable. I felt as if God was saying to me, 'I gave my Son—for *you*—what are you going to do about it?' And I wasn't at all sure how to answer Him.

Suddenly, as we were kneeling there I felt Nicky nudge me in the ribs.

'God gave His Son for the world', she hissed, 'and that means *you*'. I edged away from her elbow, and continued to think. Finally I struck a bargain with God.

'If you want me to give my life to You and be a Christian', I said to Him, 'I'll tell You what I'll do. I'll watch and listen to everything that my sister does and says for the next two weeks, and if she lets You down—well, I shall know that the Christian life is not the one for me. If I am going to be a Christian I've got to be sure that You can make me strong enough to be a good one'.

I was absolutely awful to Nicky during the next two weeks. I aggravated her in every possible way. I took the opposite side of every argument, borrowed her things without asking her, and teased her about being a Christian. She came through with flying colours.

At the end of the fortnight I went down on my knees at the evening service at the Army and prayed something like this:

'All right, Lord, you've proved your point. If you really want me—you can have me. But please help me not to let you down'.

When you've made up your mind to be a Christian at an Army service, you go forward to a special form

that stands at the front, and kneel down. That's to show everyone that now you're on God's side. It takes a bit of courage to walk down there in front of everybody, but an officer comes and kneels with you for company, which helps a lot.

The Captain in charge of the meeting talked to me afterwards and told me I mustn't be afraid of people knowing that I had made up my mind to follow Christ.

'Tell your mother, your friends and the people you work with', he said. 'It's much easier if you make the position clear right from the beginning'.

When I told my mother she just laughed.

'It won't last long with you', she said; 'Nothing ever does. Nicky, yes—but not you'.

I really was mad at her, but I didn't say anything. I knew it was the first test I had had over controlling my temper, but I was boiling inside.

'I'll just show you!' I muttered to myself. 'I'll just show you that it will last—you see if I don't'.

It was my first challenge and I accepted it gladly.

If you want to become a Salvationist you have to go to classes. They last for eight weeks and the officer who takes them makes sure that you really understand what it means to be a Christian. You are told about being an example to others, and you're expected to give up smoking and drinking as well. The classes also include instruction regarding Salvation Army procedure and principles.

At the end of eight weeks I became a member of the Salvation Army, and at the same time I left the dairy and went to work at the laundry with Nicky. I had become fed up with the long cycle ride to work every day and the laundry was closer, and besides I'd have Nicky for company. But somehow the change didn't satisfy me. The work seemed pointless. Oh, I knew that for health reasons it was a good thing for people to have clean towels every day—but it was such discouraging work. Towels that went out clean one day came back dirty the next, and the whole boring routine of washing, and ironing, and rolling, and packing, just went on over and over again.

A friend of mine was a Sister at Cirencester Hospital. One evening I was telling her about being fed up with my job and wanting a change, and she came up with a surprising suggestion.

'Why don't you train as a State Enrolled Nurse?' she said. 'If you get on OK you could then have a try at becoming a fully State Registered Nurse'.

I had never thought about becoming a nurse before, but somehow the idea sounded interesting. I applied for training, was accepted and went to the Preliminary Training School at Lacock in Wiltshire to start my course. I found that I enjoyed it very much. Three months of my training was in a Maternity Hospital in Cirencester, and I enjoyed that most of all. When I finished my training I decided to go back to the Maternity Hospital, and I worked there for eighteen months. I loved working with the mothers and babies, and it was much more satisfying work than canning milk or laundering towels!

My friend Ruth had by this time trained to become a full-time Salvation Army Officer. She had been at the William Booth Memorial College at Denmark Hill, in London. Nicky was there too, and in 1962 Ruth invited me to her Commissioning service which was held in the Albert Hall.

During the evening gathering God spoke to me very clearly.

'Jeanette', He said—not in a loud voice that everyone could hear, of course, but quietly, inside my mind. 'Jeanette—I want you to be a full time Salvation Army Officer too'.

I just couldn't believe it.

'You can't mean it, Lord!' I said. 'What have I got to offer?'

Once God has started to speak to you about something like that, you can never quite forget about it. Time after time the call to be a full time Salvation Army Officer came to the front of my mind, and time after time I pushed it to the back again.

I have forgotten to tell you that I had become engaged by now. My fiancé was a boy from Stroud —a member of the Salvation Army as well. Perhaps one of the reasons that I wouldn't listen to God's voice was because I had a nasty feeling that if I went into full-time service it would mean breaking off my engagement. My fiancé had a good steady job in Stroud, and he had not received any special call from God to enter the Army full time.

One evening I went to a big Salvation Army meeting at Bristol and a high ranking officer made a special appeal.

'We desperately need men and women who are prepared to dedicate their whole lives in service to God', he said, and it was then that I knew I couldn't put off a decision any longer.

'All right, God', I said. 'If You are so determined —take my life—and use it as You want to'.

That weekend I told my fiancé of my decision. We were both very upset. It's not easy to make a break with someone you love, and give up the immediate idea of having a home and family of your own. My fiancé was very understanding.

'I always knew that you had got to put this first, Jeanette', he admitted, and somehow that made things a little easier.

I enrolled at Denmark Hill College in 1963—the year that Nicky left as a fully-trained officer.

We moved around a lot during our training. I went to the Eventide Home in Godalming which is for old people, and also spent some time at a girl's training home at Southsea. I wasn't madly keen about either of them!

'This isn't the kind of work for me', I thought. 'I only hope the Lord knows what He is doing'.

I was quite glad to get back to college again. We learned about the Goodwill Department of the Salvation Army, which involves visiting old and needy people in their homes; the evangelistic side which covers learning to run meetings, take open air services and teach in Sunday School; and the social services side which covers all kinds of service to the people around you who need help.

A Commissioner was in charge of the Men's social services and he impressed me very much with his true stories of helping people through the Salvation Army's residential work—where men, women, young people and children, actually live in homes run by the Army so that they are helped through their difficulties, and learn about the Lord Jesus Christ at the same time.

'I wonder if I could do something like that', I wondered. 'Show me, Lord, if that is what you want me to do'.

The idea kept coming back to my mind time after time, and in February 1964 when I was interviewed by the lady Colonel, I asked for my name to be placed on the Women's social services list. In May I was appointed to the Mother and Baby Home in Bristol for a period of two and a half months. By this time I had got quite used to answering to the title of 'Cadet'. At Bristol I helped in the general running of the home and looked after the mothers and babies. We had a Major who was Warden of the Home, a Major who was Homemother, and two Captains who were in charge of the medical side of the work.

In 1964 I was moved to a Girls' Probation Home in Cheltenham. Girls who have misbehaved in some way—such as by stealing, or running away from home, were sent to a Salvation Army Home for a year in order to be taught how to live better and fuller lives. I was at Cheltenham for two months as a Cadet but I didn't enjoy it very much, and I was very pleased when during my Passing Out Service in the Albert Hall on May 14th, 1965, I heard the words:

'Cadet Jeanette, you are promoted to the rank of Lieutenant and appointed to Marshfield Children's Home in Southport'.

I went off to Southport feeling very excited, for I was about to take up my first position as a fully trained, full time uniformed and commissioned Salvation Army Officer. I was met at the station by a Major in a minibus and taken to the children's home. The children were of all ages from two to 15 and I was put in charge of 14 of them. There were about 35 children in the home and they were divided into three family groups, with an officer to look after each group. The baby of my group was called Sharon, and she sat in her high chair in the dining-

room looking at me across the table with great interest. I wondered if she somehow knew that I was going to be her 'mother' for the next few months.

The days at Marshfield were full and busy ones. We had to do all the washing and ironing for the children in our charge, take them backwards and forwards to school in the minibus, and clean certain rooms in the house each day, just as an ordinary mother would have to do.

I enjoyed my time at Marshfield very much. Somehow I managed to squeeze driving lessons into my spare time, and I was very thrilled when I finally passed my driving test.

In November 1967 I was promoted to Captain, and moved back to the Mother and Baby Home in Bristol where I had first worked as a Cadet. I only did part-time duties in the Home—the rest of the time I was official driver for a District Officer. Her area stretched over Plymouth, Bath, Weston and Cardiff, so I got around quite a bit.

You may think that once I became a Salvation Army Officer I had no more trouble with my quick temper. Well, you would be wrong! Although I was, of course, learning to control it most of the time, I can remember one time in particular when it nearly got me into trouble again.

One of the girls in the Bristol Home was supposed to be cleaning a room, but when I went to see how she was getting on I found she had put down her broom and duster, and was dancing to the radio—

which she had turned on full.

'Please turn off that radio', I said pleasantly, 'and get on with your work. It's nearly time this room was finished'.

The girl turned on me with flashing eyes. Some of the girls were pretty tough types and this one was no exception.

'Don't get me riled', she threatened, sticking her face up close to mine.

'I'm not "getting you riled",' I replied patiently, taking a step backwards, 'I'm just asking you to get your work done'.

With that the girl moved up to me quickly, and without any warning, smacked me hard across the face. For a moment I saw red, and my hand started to move upwards to hit her back. But, do you know, it was as if someone had got hold of my hand and refused to let it go—however hard I tugged. I believe it was God!

I turned and went out of the room without saying anything.

Later the girl came and apologized.

'You don't know how near you were to getting your face slapped in return', I told her. 'The only reason I didn't hit you back was because I am a Christian—and God has told us that we are not to hit people back when they hit us, but to turn the other cheek. It was God holding my hand so that I didn't hit you'.

The girl was quite amazed.

'I'll never do it again, Captain, I promise you',

she said. And she never did. That girl really changed and became quite different afterwards, and to me it seemed that the change started on that day.

In 1969 the Mother and Baby Home in Bristol closed down and I waited eagerly to learn of my next posting. My heart sank when it finally arrived. I was to be sent to the Probation Home at Cheltenham again. I hadn't enjoyed my stay at Cheltenham when I went there for two months as a Cadet, and I knew that the officer in charge thought I lacked confidence in myself, and would never be suitable for girls' work. However, in the Army when you are sent somewhere you don't argue, and so off to Cheltenham I went.

Have you noticed that things are often not as bad as you expect them to be? I wasn't at all pleased with the idea of going back to Cheltenham, but when I settled down I found I liked it much better than I had expected. I was older, of course, and more sure of myself, and I was a Captain now and not just a Cadet.

I stayed at Cheltenham for over two years and then found myself on the move again. First I went to a girls' probation home in London, and from there I was sent to an Approved School in Yorkshire.

I work with problem teenage girls at the school. They have training in cleaning, washing, mending, etc., as well as a full time education. Various educational trips are arranged too. We try to teach the girls by word and action a better way of living, and by trying to understand them we aim at introducing them to Jesus who can be their friend.

I really like my work in Yorkshire, and I never have time to feel fed up or bored. I'm very glad I gave my life to the Lord that night in the Salvation Army Gospel Hall when I was 17, and I'm glad He called me to serve Him full-time in the Salvation Army when I was older.

Next time you see a girl in a Salvation Army bonnet, will you think of me, and find time to pray for me and the girls I am trying to help up here in Yorkshire?